Becoming The Mind-Reading Parent

A Step-By-Step Guide for Parenting Kids with Anxiety – Stopping the Worry Cycle and Improving Your Kids' Courage (Help Them Grow into Independent Individuals)

Martha B. Bailey

Bluesource And Friends

This book is brought to you by Bluesource And Friends, a happy book publishing company.

Our motto is **"Happiness Within Pages"**

We promise to deliver amazing value to readers with our books.

We also appreciate honest book reviews from our readers.

Connect with us on our Facebook page www.facebook.com/bluesourceandfriends and stay tuned to our latest book promotions and free giveaways.

Becoming The Mind Reading Parent

Don't forget to claim your FREE books!

Brain Teasers:

https://tinyurl.com/karenbrainteasers

Harry Potter Trivia:

https://tinyurl.com/wizardworldtrivia

Sherlock Puzzle Book (Volume 2)

https://tinyurl.com/Sherlockpuzzlebook2

Becoming The Mind Reading Parent

Also check out our other books

"67 Lateral Thinking Puzzles"
https://tinyurl.com/thinkingandriddles

"Rookstorm Online Saga"
https://tinyurl.com/rookstorm

"Korman's Prayer"
https://tinyurl.com/kormanprayer

"The Convergence"
https://tinyurl.com/bloodcavefiction

"The Hardest Sudokos In Existence (Ranked As The Hardest Sudoku Collection Available In The Western World)"
https://tinyurl.com/MasakiSudoku

Becoming The Mind Reading Parent

Table of Contents

Description 9

Introduction.. 12

Chapter 1: Anxiety is Not an Illness 16

Understanding Anxiety.. 18

What Is Considered "Normal" Anxiety for a Child?
.... 19

Do Thoughts and Feelings Contribute Toward
Anxiety? 22

Chapter 2: Different Types of Anxiety...................... 26

Familiarize Yourself with the Different Types of
Anxiety.. 27

How Do I Determine if My Child Has Anxiety? . 32

What Triggers My Child's Anxiety?........................ 35

Chapter 3: *You* Need to Remain Calm First 38

What to Do When Your Child's Anxiety is Making
You Nervous.. 38

Becoming The Mind Reading Parent

Parenting Your Anxious Child While Effectively Remaining Calm 39

What *Not* to Do When Parenting an Anxious Child 45

Parents, You Need to Relax, Too 47

Chapter 4: Observing Your Actions 51

Am I Contributing to My Child's Fears? 52

What You Should *Never* Say to an Anxious Child 55

Helpful Words to Use When Parenting Your Anxious Child 60

Chapter 5: Why Do Kids Worry Anyway?................. 62

Understanding the Reasons behind the Worry..... 63

How Worry Grows and Why it Needs to Go....... 68

Chapter 6: Observing What Your Kids Do............... 72

What Every Parent with an Anxious Child Should Know 72

Watching for Signs of Anxiety 75

Becoming The Mind Reading Parent

Chapter 7: Decluttering Media and Technology 81

Could Technology be Causing Anxiety? 81

Reconnecting with Your Digitally-Distracted Child

.... 84

Chapter 8: Nighttime Pillow Talk 89

Strategies to Help Calm Your Child at Night 90

Important Words that Help You Connect with

Your Child Before Bed 95

Chapter 9: Morning Talks to Promote Positive

Thinking 99

Establish a Routine that Encourages Positive

Thinking 100

How to Foster Positive Thinking to Help Your

Child Overcome Anxiety 103

Chapter 10: Facing Their Fears (Gradually) 107

Chapter 11: Eat, Pray, Sleep, and Exercise 115

Eating Right for a Healthy Mind 116

Sleeping Soundly at Night..118

The Gift of Exercise..119

And Finally, the Power of Prayer............................122

Conclusion 124

Description

Could my child really be affected by anxiety?

Absolutely. Everyone, both young and old, is capable of experiencing anxiety. When your fears become so strong, so intense, powerful, and overwhelming that they prevent you from being able to function normally, and they cause extreme levels of distress – that is anxiety.

Every parent wants nothing but the best for their child, but how do they do that when it's breaking their heart to see their child struggling with anxiety? What is worse is feeling helpless about what they could do to help them. Phobias, being withdrawn from social settings, separation anxiety, and obsessive-compulsive behavior patterns are symptoms of anxiety that could hold your child back. These symptoms can rob them of childhood

Becoming The Mind Reading Parent

happiness that you long for them to experience. It doesn't always have to be like that. As the parent, you're in a unique position of being able to do something about it.

"Becoming the Mind-Reading Parent: A Step-By-Step Guide for Parenting Kids with Anxiety, Stopping the Worry Cycle, and Improving Your Kids' Courage (Help Them Grow into Independent Individuals)" provides a straightforward, simple, and effective approach that will help parents guide their young children and teenagers struggling with anxiety. This book can help your child to grow into happy, confident, and resilient adults. It will walk you through the solutions that you need to alleviate your child's fears and the things that you can do to stop aggravating their condition without realizing it. Understanding your child's anxiety is the first and most important step in helping them overcome the internal struggles that they face every day. Your child may not know how to cope yet, and that's where you can come in and make the difference.

This book will walk you through:

- Why anxiety is not an illness
- Understanding the different types of anxiety
- Why it is important for *parents* to remain calm
- How to observe your own actions
- Phrases you should *never* say to your anxious child
- Understand why kids worry
- How to encourage your child to gradually face their fears
- Digitally decluttering and reconnecting with your child
- And more...

Don't let anxiety rob your child of their happiness. A happy childhood *is possible*, and it begins right now.

Introduction

Congratulations on downloading this book, and thank you for doing so.

With one in ten children and adolescents experiencing an anxiety disorder, this has become one of the most common mental health conditions in the world. While anxiety on its own is not an illness, but is, in fact, a normal part of the many ranges of emotions we experience as a person, anxiety disorder is considered a mental health condition because it needs help and treatment before it can be resolved.

All children will experience anxiety. They are young, growing, and learning, and some new experiences are bound to make them nervous, worried, and even a little bit anxious. Certain types of worries and fears are perfectly normal, depending on their age group. It is common for the younger children to be afraid of the dark, of strangers, or even of loud noises. Most children will grow out of their fears as they get older, so there is nothing to worry about. However, you need to pay attention if these fears become so big that your child finds it hard to function daily. When they find it hard to calm down, concentrate, or even partake in social activities, that is the time when anxiety becomes a disorder that might need some medical attention.

Why is it so important to get these children the help that they need? Unlike fully grown adults, children do not know how to work through their feelings and process them. Even some adults have not fully grasped the best technique to manage their emotions and channel them in healthy ways – children will find it even more difficult. They do not always understand why they feel the way that they do, which is why anxiety is a condition that will continue to prevail into adolescence and for the rest of their lives if nothing is done about it. In more severe cases, untreated anxiety can eventually lead to depression, and possibly even substance abuse.

Not all anxious children end up getting the help that they need, as many parents often do not notice the signs soon enough to recognize that anxiety is a problem. Some parents might believe that their child will eventually grow out of that behavior, not realizing that the condition could become even more debilitating. Then there are others who simply think that that kind of behavior is normal, especially if they, too, behave in a similar manner. As a result, many parents who are dealing with children struggling with anxiety often find themselves at a loss about what to do.

Well, the good news is, you have taken the first important step in the right direction by picking up this book. The practical tools and strategies found in

Becoming The Mind Reading Parent

the next several chapters will help you recognize, manage, and support your child to cope with anxiety, whether they are only just beginning to reveal symptoms of the condition, or they have already been diagnosed with an anxiety disorder. Finding out information about the topic will help both you and your child work through the condition so that their childhood will not have to be compromised.

There are plenty of books on this subject on the market, so thanks again for choosing this one! Every effort was made to ensure it is full of as much useful information as possible. Please, enjoy!

Chapter 1: Anxiety is Not an Illness

Anxiety is not an illness. Let us be clear about that from the beginning. Yes, to a certain extent, if it is experienced on more severe levels, anxiety can be classified as a medical condition which may require professional help, but it is *not an illness*. Anxiety is just one of the many emotions all of us experience as humans. Adults go through it. Teenagers go through it. Even children do feel anxious from time to time. In the days of the early humans, these anxious feelings were precisely the emotion that was so crucial to their survival. It kept them alert toward the dangers around them, and it warned them of any incoming predators. It also made them attentive while they were out hunting for food.

Anxiety can be accompanied by physical symptoms, which include an increase in heart rate, heightened alertness to the surroundings, and even sweating, on some occasions. This heightened sensitivity would then produce a rush of adrenaline. In the early days, this triggered the "fight or flight" response mechanism toward an adversary. This mechanism continues to remain in all of us to this very day. It may not be as strong as it was when humans lived centuries ago, but we still feel traces of it in our lives in certain situations.

Feeling nervous before a big announcement is typical. Feeling anxious enough to be concerned for your safety as you look both ways before crossing the street is normal. Feeling nervous before having to make an important presentation at work is normal. Feeling anxious about being pushed out of your comfort zone and going through a new experience is normal. Again, anxiety is not an illness, but when it reaches a certain level where it starts to disrupt your ability to function, then it becomes a problem that might require medical attention. When it reaches that stage, it then becomes what is known as an "anxiety disorder".

Understanding Anxiety

Contrary to what you might think, it is normal for both adults and children to feel anxious. You might even say that it is considered healthy on some levels. It is only when anxiety is experienced on disproportionate levels that it becomes a problem. Forty million people in just the United States alone are affected by anxiety. Out of that number, only 36.9% are receiving treatment for it, according to the Anxiety and Depression Association of America.

Defining what "anxiety" means, the American Psychological Association (APA) refers to it as an emotion which is characterized by certain feelings that include tension and having worried thoughts. One may also experience physical changes to the body, such as an increase in blood pressure.

Both adults and children are just as likely to experience anxiety. Being able to differentiate between when your child is feeling a reasonable amount of anxiety and when they might require medical attention is the key to getting your child the help that they need.

What Is Considered "Normal" Anxiety for a Child?

Being afraid of certain things is a common behavior among young children. They are at an age when they are still learning and processing the world around them. Certain new experiences might make them nervous or even a little afraid because it is unfamiliar to them. However, most children learn to cope and adapt to new experiences with time.

Becoming The Mind Reading Parent

However, if you do notice that your child seems to be feeling more anxious than the other children their age, they might be experiencing anxiety that requires more support to help them cope with it. This is also true when they become so anxious that they stop wanting to participate in school or other social interactions. If their anxiety starts to interfere with their ability to get things done as compared to the other children of the same age, they might need some help.

Anxiety does not just affect how your child feels, but the way that they think as well. From birth to 8 years are the years when most of their learning and development take place. This is also a very crucial period when having anxious thoughts can have a significant impact on them as they grow into adulthood. Children who have not been given the proper support or coping mechanisms to work through their emotions could carry their anxiety with them into adulthood.

Children who are dealing with anxiety tend to perceive danger or fear to be greater than it is. The more they think about it, the worse it seems to make them feel. Some children could start to form their own coping mechanism to manage these distressing scenarios. Most of the time, one of their coping mechanisms involves the preference of avoiding the situation entirely. Or, they could turn to their parents for help and ask them to deal with it for them.

While it may be a good start to observe them developing their own strategies and trying to solve their problems on their own, this kind of strategy, unfortunately, will not work in the long run. If their solution is always to try to avoid the problem, they will likely avoid facing or managing the same situation when it repeats itself. As time goes on, they will find it harder to handle daily stressful emotions that come with school, social environments, and their home. Problematic anxiety very seldom goes away or resolves itself, and unless children are taught from the very beginning how to overcome or cope with these overwhelming emotions, they are very likely to struggle with anxiety for the rest of their life.

The kind of anxiety that is problematic is not a lifelong condition, but it can persist for as long as a person's entire life because those who struggle with it do not understand how anxiety affects their body. In addition, they do not seek the help that they need.

Do Thoughts and Feelings Contribute Toward Anxiety?

Children get frightened and worried, too. Being anxious or scared sometimes is all part of the experience as they grow into adulthood. <u>One in four</u>

children experiences childhood anxiety when they are between 13 and 18 years old. In that age group, there is a 6% chance that some of those children will experience anxiety for life. If the children do not receive the help that they need, this can eventually lead to problems at home, school, and among their peers. They will also experience issues in their adult life. The exact causes of childhood anxiety are not known definitively, but studies show that an anxious child's brain tends to behave a little differently than the brain of an average child.

It is difficult to pinpoint the exact kind of thoughts or feelings a child might have that could contribute to their anxiety. The reason for this is that anxiety is caused by a range of factors, and not just a single one: To a certain extent, anxiety can be caused by genetics. It could even be a parental influence, where a child picks up this characteristic and develops the same behavior patterns from a parent who also experiences anxiety. It could also be caused by an overactive amygdala, which is the structural part of the brain that contributes to how a person responds to fear and which controls the feelings of anxiety. Other times, anxious thoughts in your child could simply stem from a past negative experience that they might have had, which makes them fearful of the prospect of going through it again.

Anxiety may also be caused by an imbalance in the body's natural chemicals. When the serotonin hormones, in particular, become imbalanced, that could contribute to the anxiety of your child, since these hormones are responsible for regulating the moods that humans experience, children included.

Given proper treatment, anxiety does not have to rob your child of their happy childhood experiences. They can learn to live full, happy, and healthy lives while learning how to develop the right coping mechanisms which will allow them to keep their anxieties under control.

Chapter 2: Different Types of Anxiety

Anxiety is not pleasant, and it certainly does not feel good having to watch your child struggle with it, wishing you could take away their pain and their fears. While it may not always feel good to a certain degree, experiencing anxiety is normal.

Not every child is going to experience anxiety in the same way. Some children experience it on more manageable levels, while others may suffer from anxiety at more profound, crippling levels. On some occasions, it could manifest as a panic attack or a nervous breakdown. Anxiety is divided into several categories, and familiarizing yourself with the different types of anxiety that your child may go through can help you develop a better understanding of what they might be experiencing. This is especially true when they face certain situations which can end up acting as triggers to their anxiety.

Familiarize Yourself with the Different Types of Anxiety

Anxiety can manifest itself in several forms, and when these types of anxieties are experienced excessively, appropriate treatment may be required to get it under control, especially if self-coping mechanisms do not seem to be doing the trick.

When anxiety starts to cause extreme worry and fear in your child to a point where it begins affecting your child's moods, sleep patterns, behavior, and even eating habits, that is classified as an anxiety disorder. Among the common types of disorders likely to be experienced by children (adults too) include the following:

- **General Anxiety Disorder (GAD).** Your child may be diagnosed with GAD if the anxiety they experience causes irritability, difficulty in concentrating in general, fatigue and poor sleep patterns, and muscle tension. GAD can cause all kinds of worries in a child. They might worry about their test scores, friendships, how well they are doing in school or sports, the relationships they have with the family, or even the weather.

- **Separation Anxiety Disorder (SAD).** Not all SAD is a cause for alarm. Depending on your child's developmental stage, it is natural for them to experience some levels of SAD, particularly those between the ages of 1 and 3. However, when older children experience it on excessive levels whenever they are being separated from their caregivers, then that might be a cause for concern. Children dealing with SAD frequently worry about being away from their parents. They may have nightmares and fears about their parents leaving them or dying, and they may refuse to go to school or anywhere without their parents. Extreme cases of SAD could manifest physically in the form of frequent headaches and nausea, and this is when your child may require medical attention if self-coping mechanisms fail to work.

- **Social Anxiety Disorder (SAD).** Another form of SAD is experienced within a social context, where your child may have an intense fear of being around others or participating in any kind of social activity. A child who is experiencing this may resort to crying, clinging to adults, throwing tantrums, and refusing to take part in any social activity.

- **Selective Mutism.** Some children may resort to what is known as selective mutism to cope with their anxiety. In social situations, they may refuse to speak, only choosing to do so when they feel comfortable enough. Selective mutism is a common diagnosis around the 5-year-old age group.

- **Specified Phobias.** Exhibiting excessive fear and alarm toward a specific object or situation, which lasts for a prolonged period, could be classified as a specified phobia. Children experiencing this could cry, freeze entirely, or cling to an adult for security.

- **Panic Disorder.** If you notice that your child experiences recurring panic attacks more frequently than they should, they could be dealing with panic disorders. Physical symptoms which might manifest in this condition include chest pains, difficulty in breathing, shortness of breath, dizziness, nausea, and possible chills or heat sensations.

- **Obsessive Compulsive Disorder (OCD).** When your child exhibits certain repeated behaviors which are unwanted and that interferes with their everyday life, that is OCD. Washing their hands excessively or being fixated on only a certain way of doing things is an example of OCD disorder. Your child may start to cry and become overly emotional if they are not able to do what they "think" they need to do.

- **Post-Traumatic Stress Disorder (PTSD).** This is commonly experienced by those who have undergone a particularly negative situation that left a profound impact on them. Children dealing with PTSD could have frequent and recurring nightmares, and sometimes their fears are so intense, it prevents them from being able to do anything else when that panic sets in.

How Do I Determine if My Child Has Anxiety?

Given that childhood is packed with many new experiences and learning opportunities, it can be hard to distinguish when your child is feeling a healthy amount of fear and when that fear begins to cross over the "anxiety" territory.

It is normal for every child to feel worried. They may worry about the monsters under their bed or what is going to happen on a test tomorrow; they may worry if they are going to make any new friends at school. If you do suspect that your child's fears may be symptoms of underlying anxiety, there are two types of signs that you should look out for. These are physical and emotional signs.

When anxiety manifests itself physically, the signs that often come with it include:

- Complaints of frequent headaches or stomach aches
- Refusal to eat when they are at school
- Refusal to use the toilet unless they are at home
- Restlessness and fidgeting
- Hyperactivity
- Being easily distracted (this often gets mistaken for ADHD)
- Sweating or trembling visibly in situations that scare them
- Constant muscle tension
- Difficulty falling asleep or staying awake

The emotional signs that you want to watch out for include:

- Frequent crying
- Becoming extremely sensitive to what is being said to them
- Being irritable or angry without a good reason
- Experiencing panic attacks
- Having phobias about certain things
- Constant worry over making mistakes
- Worrying about what others might think
- Refusing to be separated from their parents and becoming extremely emotional when they need to be
- Being distracted from something (For example, they would stop playing entirely if they are worried about something.)
- Constantly asking "what if something bad happens"? (Their questions tend to center around a negative outcome.)
- Evasion of social settings
- Refusal to go to school

- Keeping to themselves most of the time instead of interacting with other kids
- Refusal to speak to strangers
- Constantly seeking approval from parents and other caregivers, or even their peers and teachers
- Getting upset over the slightest thing
- Worrying all the time
- Clinging to their parents, especially among younger children
- Always asking their parents or caregivers for help on certain things, even though they know how to do those things by themselves
- Refusal to go to sleep without an adult present

What Triggers My Child's Anxiety?

Aside from the biological factors which were discussed in Chapter 1 as possible causes for your child's anxiety, there are several other triggers which might cause them to experience this emotion. Some children are more easily affected than others because of the simple fact that every child is different. It does not mean that there is something ''wrong' with them; it could only be part of their personality make up.

- **Their Environment.** If your child has undergone a traumatic experience such as divorce or death in the family, this could act as an anxiety trigger.

- **Stress.** Excessive stress could be a trigger for anxiety in a child. Parents need to remember that children do not process their feelings in the same way that adults do. What an adult thinks is normal might be an experience which is stressful for the child.

- **Medical Reasons.** Autism spectrum disorder and ADHD could be partly the trigger for your child's anxiety, given that these underlying medical conditions would cause their brain to function differently.

- **Inability to Cope.** Parents might forget that older children still may not necessarily have the right coping mechanism to work through their emotions. Being unable to cope with their overwhelming feelings could also be a potential anxiety trigger that often gets overlooked.

- **Personal Triggers.** Reliving bad memories or bad experiences in their mind and not knowing quite what to do with it is another potential anxiety trigger. Whenever you notice that your child is deep in thought with a worried look on their face, they could be replaying scenarios in their head, which might be feeding into their fears.

Chapter 3: *You* Need to Remain Calm First

Even the most patient and well-meaning parents can experience bouts of frustration and anger when a child is being anxious and acting up because of it. No parent wants to see their child suffer. But, in trying to protect your child, you could actually be doing them more harm than good by exacerbating their anxiety. In your effort to keep them safe and shield them from their emotions, you could end up being just as anxious yourself. You may feel completely helpless because you do not know what to do to make things better.

What to Do When Your Child's Anxiety is Making You Nervous

Whenever you see your child having an anxiety episode, try not to be too hard on yourself. Most parents tend to feel as if they have failed their child as a parent because they could not protect them or shield them from their own fears. Anxiety disorder is not a reflection of your parenting style – not in the least – and blaming yourself will only add more stress on you, your child, and the rest of the family.

What you need to aim for here, instead, is to try to build a supportive network that both you and your anxious child can lean on. Support can come in the form of family, friends, and even external services that are specifically set up to help families work through situations like these.

Parenting Your Anxious Child While Effectively Remaining Calm

A parent's natural instinct is having the desire to protect their child when they see them going into a heightened state of anxiety. As a parent, you may attempt to help your child by trying to solve their problem. Or, you would want them to avoid issues by keeping them away from triggers. You also may try to create a lifestyle that is stress-free and does not promote worrying. While these various approaches are certainly a positive step in the right direction, parents still need to understand that they simply cannot prevent their child from going through anxiety. It is part of our range of human emotions, and being able to navigate this emotion is part of developing essential life skills which will help them overcome challenges later in life. You may not be able to stop it, but you can certainly teach your child to learn how to manage it.

In these anxious moments, the best thing you can do is to remain calm throughout your child's anxiety episode. Be the voice of reason, the support, and the calming presence that your child needs. It is not going to help the child if you wear your distress on your sleeve, too – that is only going to make them feel even *more* anxious than ever. Get a handle on your own emotions first, and then begin working through these steps with your child.

- **Stop, Breathe, Reassure.** Reassuring your child is not as simple as telling them that there is nothing to be afraid of. The reason that their anxiety does not seem to go away even when you say there is nothing to fear is that even though they *want* to listen, their brain is not letting that happen. During bouts of anxiety, the prefrontal cortex of the brain, which is responsible for logic and reason, gets put on pause while the more emotional part of the brain rapidly takes over. It is hard for your child to think logically or clearly in these moments. Instead of telling them, "everything's going to be okay," get them to stop and look at you. Encourage your child to take deep breaths together with you. While they continue to breathe, express empathy by letting them know you understand how frightening this must be for them. Once the deep breathing has helped them settle down, talk with your child. Give them possible suggestions that might help them feel better in this situation.

- **Let Them Know that Worrying is Normal.** An older child experiencing anxiety might have moments when they wonder what is wrong with them and why they are like this. From the moment you notice that your child is struggling with anxiety, no matter what age they may be, reassure them, and let them know there is absolutely nothing wrong with them. Tell them that worrying is entirely normal, and everyone worries from time to time. In fact, this is a good opportunity for you to teach your child the reasons behind their worries. You could even make a little game out of it by teaching them to play detective by trying to figure out their own triggers.

- **Create a Worry Ritual.** Getting your child to embrace their worries is part of the coping mechanism of learning how to deal with anxiety. It also helps to reassure them not to feel guilty or as if there is something wrong with them whenever they do. A good exercise that parents can do together with their child is creating a "worry ritual" as part of their daily routine. Sit down with your child for 15 minutes a day, and encourage your child to talk freely about their worries. They could draw it out, talk about it, or even write it down – for the older kids.

- **Create Small Goals.** Allowing your child to avoid everything that makes them anxious is not a healthy coping mechanism. In fact, avoidance is going to have the opposite effect, which will eventually make your child's anxiety worse. Instead of encouraging them when they want to avoid something, help them break it down into smaller, more manageable goals that they can work on. If your child is afraid of falling off the swing, for example, instead of keeping them away from the parks, work with them on smaller goals that they would be comfortable doing. Perhaps today, their small goal would be going to the park without going near the swing. Next week, when they are more comfortable in the park, the next goal could be to touch the swing. Eventually, when they have worked up the courage, encourage them to sit on the swing. Allowing them time to

develop the confidence they need to
overcome their fears will give them the
confidence to get past other challenges with
the same approach.

What *Not* to Do When Parenting an Anxious Child

Parents can sometimes be so focused on trying to keep their child safe and aiming for the anxiety to go away that they end up making several mistakes along the way. Sometimes, this does not only make their child's anxiety worse, but it also goes so far as to make the child feel worse and diminish their confidence. As challenging as it might be to watch your child go through anxiety, remember to avoid the following mistakes when parenting an anxious child:

Becoming The Mind Reading Parent

- Avoid overprotecting them, as this prevents them from learning how to deal with life's difficulties, especially when they get older.

- Avoid expressing anger, frustration, or criticism – these reactions are not helpful at all for your anxious child.

- Avoid telling your child that they are unreasonable or ridiculous – your child needs support and empathy.

- Avoid trying to dismiss their anxiety, because failing to accept the reality of the situation is only going to make them more frustrated and miserable.

- Avoid dismissing your child – they need to feel that bond and connection with you more than ever when they are feeling anxious.

- Avoid reinforcing your child's fears with avoidance.

Parents, You Need to Relax, Too

Parenting an anxious child is not easy, and the intensity of the emotions experienced can take its toll, not just on your child but on you too. As important as it is to get your child to relax and calm down, you need to make time for yourself to recharge emotionally as well. Stress can be overwhelming and wear you out physically and mentally. Being the best parent that you can be means that you need to take care of yourself first before you can effectively take care of others.

Breathing deeply, for example, is not just a relaxation technique that is effective for your child, but is also good for you. Whenever you find yourself feeling particularly stressed out, taking a few moments to close your eyes, pause, and focus on nothing but your deep breaths can do wonders to alleviate your stress. You can also achieve this if you picture the tension leaving your body with each exhalation and feel your body get lighter with each breath.

Meditation is another favorite relaxation technique that has been around for centuries, and the reason it has endured for so long is demonstrated by the wealth of benefits associated with this practice. Just a few minutes of meditation every day is all it takes to center yourself and find your focus again. Research has even suggested that the benefits of meditating regularly could alter the neural pathways in your brain, which eventually makes you even more resilient toward stress. This is one practice you could even do with your child. Encourage them to sit with you and meditate to a positive mantra. Guided meditations are especially useful, providing cues and walking you through the process so you can get the most out of your experience.

Becoming The Mind Reading Parent

Sometimes, the best remedy for a stressful day could be to reach out and talk to someone about it. Talk to your spouse, friend, or another family member, and simply share what is going on with you and how you feel. Getting it off your chest and receiving support in return can make you feel much better.

If relaxation alone works best for you, try the decompress-and-relax method. Simply take a warm compress or a heat wrap and place it around your shoulders and neck for the next 10 to 15 minutes. Then lie back in a comfortable position, play some soothing tunes on your mobile phone, and close your eyes. Allow yourself to relax completely as you visualize the tension leaving your body. Breathe deeply throughout as you let the warmth of the compress permeate your tired muscles.

Finally, there is nothing more relaxing for your mind, body, and soul than to laugh out loud. Laugh genuinely, laugh deeply, and feel how your body transforms when you do. Laugh with your family, laugh with your kids, and laugh with your friends. Fill your life and your child's with as much laughter as possible to remind yourself that, even in the most stressful situations and despite you or your child's anxiety, life is good. This would remind you that there are plenty of reasons to count your blessings and be grateful every day.

Chapter 4: Observing Your Actions

It is normal for kids to feel scared or afraid sometimes. Even as adults, we get nervous, worried, or anxious about what we do not know or what we may not be familiar with. It is the same thing with kids, and as they grow, what they are afraid or anxious about changes along the way.

Even children as young as infants experience fear. Infants may display fear in the form of being anxious over strangers and unfamiliar faces. Toddlers may feel anxious at the thought of being separated from their parents. Between the ages of 4 and 6, when a child's imagination is at its peak, they could even develop anxiety over "pretend" things or things that are not real. That is because the power of their imagination is so strong that it may not be real to us, but it is *very* real to them. Older children may experience fear and anxiety over the everyday dangers that they may encounter in real life. They could be afraid that robbers might get into the house or that natural disasters might strike. They may even worry about getting lost in a mall and that they are unable to find their parents. Preteens and teenagers feel anxious over the social pressures they face in school, their looks, or an important exam. What your child is nervous or anxious about may not always remain the same; it evolves as they grow. Anxiety is always going to be present, and overcoming one's anxiety in the past does not mean that a new one is not going to develop, which is why coping mechanisms are going to work much better than avoidance.

Am I Contributing to My Child's Fears?

You could be contributing to your child's fears if you are an anxious person yourself. While anxiety does

Becoming The Mind Reading Parent

tend to run in the family, there is still not enough underline evidence to suggest that it is primarily inherited. This then implies that perhaps the reason that your child tends to worry so much could be due to environmental factors. One such factor is their relationship with their parents and interactions that they have at home.

There is a saying that goes, *"anxious mothers will go on to make anxious children,"* which has more than a sliver of truth behind it. It is not just mothers but fathers too, and even anxious caregivers. Children are extremely observant creatures, and even when you *think* they are not paying attention, they notice what is happening around them. While parents are not deliberately trying to transfer all their anxious feelings onto their child, nervousness can still get conveyed across through your behavior. Anxious parents are more likely to be helicopter parents when they are worried, as opposed to a parent who is calmly in control of their emotions.

Becoming The Mind Reading Parent

Your intentions may be good, but excessive involvement could backfire and instead serve to increase your child's perception of danger and fear, causing them to worry even more.

Anxious parents run the risk of being *too involved* in their child's life, which is just as bad as not being involved enough. Being over-involved can lead your child to feel inadequate. They may also lack confidence in their own decisions and have the inability to get things done. They will always feel the need to seek assurance if you are constantly swooping in and trying to do things for them.

When it comes to what might cause or contribute to your child's anxiety from the parental side of things, there is no single factor that it can boil down to. It could be a combination of several factors that lead toward anxiety, and it is not just because a parent may be too involved, anxious, or overprotective. Parents who are detached and hostile also run the risk of contributing to a child's anxiety. Parents who are far too critical, negative, cynical, or excessively worrying could contribute to their anxiety too. There is also a risk of childhood anxiety being triggered in the homes of single parents.

There is no single deciding factor for this, and as parents, all you can do is your best to be as loving and supportive as possible to your child. Have a close bond and interpersonal relationship with them without being too involved. Be encouraging, and most importantly, be there to listen with empathy to your child when they need you the most.

What You Should *Never* Say to an Anxious Child

When your child is anxious, it means that they are scared. They feel completely helpless and as though they are losing control. It can sometimes be hard for parents and other caregivers to put themselves in the child's shoes, which is why they struggle to respond with two of the most essential tools that a child needs —*empathy and kindness.*

One of the many ways that parents potentially contribute to child anxiety is when they end up saying the wrong thing. What you say and what a child hears are different things. The way you communicate with your child during these crucial moments is going to determine whether you make their anxiety better or worse. In Chapter 3, you learned what not to do when parenting an anxious child, but you also need to learn what *not* to say. These are some of the things you might want to avoid saying to prevent the situation from getting worse.

- **You are the only one who is anxious.** This is only going to make your child feel even worse about themselves. If the other kids are not scared and they are, they are going to believe that there is something wrong with them after all.

- **Look at your brother/sister/friends – they are okay. Why are you scared?** This is a phrase that kills confidence. What is worse is that it will start a behavior pattern of comparison that your child might carry with them for the rest of their lives. Constantly comparing themselves to others, wondering why they are never good enough is not going to help their anxiety in any way.

- **Do not be such a worry wart.** Your intentions may be to alleviate the situation with some light humor or teasing, but this has the potential to backfire in a big way by making them feel ashamed or ridiculed, which is never a good feeling.

- **Just calm down already.** You wouldn't ask a child with a fever to stand up and just get better, would you? Asking your anxious child just to calm down makes them feel poorly about themselves, believing that their anxiety is annoying you.

- **Oh, here we go again.** Your poor child is already feeling bad about themselves for being scared and not knowing why or how to deal with it. Using phrases like these that convey your annoyance or frustration is only going to make them feel worse, and they will end up blaming themselves for their poor behavior.

- **Just think happy thoughts.** That is just putting pressure on your child, and when they fail to do it because they can't focus on anything except their fear, they will believe that there is something wrong with them.

- **You should be grateful; other kids have it worse.** Words like these make your child feel as if their feelings do not matter, and they will end up feeling guilty for being afraid, which is not going to be healthy for their emotional and mental well-being.

- **You'll be fine. Stop worrying; it's no big deal.** This is just another case of being dismissive instead of supportive. Your child is looking to you for support, and being denied of that might make them spiral downward even more.

Helpful Words to Use When Parenting Your Anxious Child

Several key sentences can make all the difference in the world to a child with anxiety. Not only do these lines make them feel the love and support they need the most, but they also help them process their emotions. And, they will gradually learn about the different coping mechanisms that can work for them.

The next time your child experiences anxiety, try the following lines instead.

- **Tell me why you are afraid. I am here to listen.**
- **Okay, I see why you are worried. Can you tell me what you think will happen next?**
- **Can you draw me a picture of what is scaring you?**
- **I love you very much; I will always do my best to keep you safe.**

Becoming The Mind Reading Parent

- Repeat after me, *"I can do this!"* We will do this as a team!
- Come, sit down with me, and let's get comfortable until the feeling goes away.
- Can you tell me how you feel? Let's learn more about that feeling.
- Let's close our eyes and picture what makes you happy.
- Can I tell you a secret? I get worried/anxious too sometimes. Everyone does; it's perfectly okay.
- I am so proud of you for being able to talk about it.
- I am so proud of you for being so brave.
- How can I help you make it better?

Chapter 5: Why Do Kids Worry Anyway?

If you are a parent of more than one child, you will notice that your childrens' temperament varies from child to child. One could be more mild-mannered and relaxed, while the other could be a crier. One could be talkative and extroverted, while another could be shy and introverted. One child could also be more anxious and tend to worry more than the other.

Anxiety is not really a problem until it begins to interfere with your child's social ability, cognitive development, and emotional growth. As adults dealing with real-world problems, you might look at a child and wonder *what on earth do they have to worry about?* Childhood is one of the simplest times in a person's life, and when all they do is play and be a child, what could they worry about?

The short answer is that anxiety is a condition that relates to the brain, and children get anxious, thanks to the pace that their brain develops. Your child's mind is most perceptive during the very early years of their life. This is when they are absorbing everything around them like a sponge, trying to make sense of it all and trying to keep up with the vast amounts of stimuli that they are exposed to every day. These include their environment, the people they meet, and the places and things that they see. It certainly does not help that the ability to cope with emotions fully develops only after adolescence, which is why teenagers are still prone to temper tantrums when they feel misunderstood.

Understanding the Reasons behind the Worry

Children, much like adults, fear and worry about the unknown. It is a natural stage of human development

– a response which is hardwired to the amygdala part of the brain. Since a child's brain experiences its fastest growth rate from birth to 8 years, fear can be magnified. This triggers their anxiety levels.

A child only begins expressing themselves once they reach the age of 3, when their vocabulary starts to pick up. By the time they reach the age of 8, they should be able to express themselves with some level of coherence. It was briefly discussed in the previous chapter how a child's worries and fears would differ throughout the various stages of their life. Let us explore that in greater detail to understand the reasons behind the worry:

- **Babies and Toddlers (Ages 0 to 2 Years).** Babies and toddlers generally experience anxiety over being separated from their parents more so than anything else. Until they reach about 10 months of age, babies tend to believe that when something is gone, it is gone forever. That is why they cry when you leave the room and can't see you anymore. As they grow older, that belief shifts, and they begin to understand that you are somewhere, even though they cannot see you. The anxiety then shifts to being afraid of being separated. This age group is also likely to feel anxious over loud noises because, at this age, their brains are extremely sensitive to sensory overload. Any loud or sudden noise could end up sending their brain into overdrive. Another common reason for worrying among kids of this age is what is known as the *external locus of control*. When your baby starts walking, they are developing a sense of independence – a feel for their surroundings. Along with this progress, their need to control their environment increases, and any element that feels beyond their control is a reason to be worried or frightened.

- **Preschoolers (Ages 3 to 5 Years).** Being afraid of the dark is a common concern of this age group because they have a hard time separating fantasy from reality (remember their imagination is at its peak during this stage). Children associate darkness with scary monsters, and they worry about being alone in the dark. Another common fear is being afraid of people dressed in costumes, like the Easter Bunny or Santa Clause. Some children simply may not be comfortable with what is unfamiliar.

- **Preteens (Ages 12 and Under).** Around this age, your child starts to worry about being at home alone by themselves. Even though they are older, they are still not confident in their ability to handle the world when Mom and Dad are not around for support. They also worry about being rejected and that something terrible might happen to the people they love. The reason for this worry lies in the fact that children are starting to understand that death is a part of life, and they begin to worry about losing the ones they love.

- **Adolescents and Teenagers (Ages 12 and Above).** Being worried about their appearance is a genuine fear that adolescents deal with because they are only now beginning to give some serious thought about their identity. As they start to understand how important social interactions are, there is an increasing need to feel accepted. They also get worried over the possibility of being embarrassed in public. In addition, during this stage, they begin to feel the pressure to perform well in school, and getting good grades becomes a cause for concern, especially when they comprehend what will happen if they failed.

How Worry Grows and Why it Needs to Go

People – children and adults alike – have a tendency to get stuck in their own heads. When this happens, it becomes difficult to move on from their worry, which allows that worry to fester and grow in their mind. This makes it seem more terrible the longer they continue to dwell on it. This happens to your child too, mainly because they do not know *how* to get out of their own heads. Fear is often described as paralyzing because it can quite literally make you feel stuck and unable to move on. Imagine that happening in the active, absorbing, and developing mind of a child, where everything seems magnified. It is no wonder that their worries continue to grow out of proportion if nothing is done to help them get through it.

Aside from potentially leading to anxiety, excessive worrying is a habit which they need to get rid of because of the other health and mental problems that are associated with it. A child that worries excessively may experience both long-term and short-term effects on their well-being. Among the short-term effects of excessive worrying include loss of sleep and indecisiveness. Some of the long-term effects could be anywhere from robbing them of happiness to physical medical conditions that are often associated with high levels of stress.

In children, excessive worrying is the most significant contributor to Generalized Anxiety Disorder (GAD), which was discussed in Chapter 2. With GAD, your child could end up worrying, obsessing, and feeling anxious about general, everyday concerns such that they find it hard to focus their mind on anything *but* their worries.

Seeing how excessive worrying can have an adverse effect on their psychological state, it is vital to help your child cope with and manage their fears. Encourage healthy coping mechanisms from a very young age instead of letting them avoid them. Helping your child keep things in perspective and not dismissing or downplaying their feelings when you do helps them develop the confidence they need, so they understand that their problems are solvable and that they have the opportunity to make themselves feel better. Not only will this increase their self-esteem over time, but it will also help your child develop necessary strength, resilience, and optimism. These are characteristics that they need to have, so they can keep standing up whenever a challenge knocks them down. This is possibly one of the most valuable life lessons a parent could teach their child.

Chapter 6: Observing What Your Kids Do

Anxiety can be just as confusing for the parents as it is for the children. You want to help your child, but sometimes you are at a loss about what to do or how to make them feel better. You are not alone, and many parents with anxiety feel precisely the same way you do. It is never easy to watch your child struggle through an ordeal.

What Every Parent with an Anxious Child Should Know

Any child can develop anxiety, just like how any child could develop diabetes, for example. It does not necessarily have to be caused by trauma either, since a lot of kids develop anxiety without trauma. A lot of parents struggle with knowing that their child has been diagnosed with an anxiety disorder. They can see

Becoming The Mind Reading Parent

that their child struggles in certain situations, but associating those struggles with anxiety is not the first thing that usually comes to mind.

Parents, this is what you need to know if you are beating yourself up about not recognizing anxiety in your child sooner: *It is going to be okay.* Yes, you do feel guilty, and you wonder how you could have missed the signs, but that is because, in all honesty, you would never *think* that it would happen to *your child.* As with most situations, a diagnosis rarely feels real until it is happening to us. You may have read all about how it is common for kids below the age of 10 to be diagnosed with anxiety, but it still does not sink in your brain that it could actually happen to your child. If there is one thing that can be guaranteed, it is that you are probably not the only parent who thought some of the struggles their child were going through were only part of growing up. After all, children are afraid of monsters under their bed, aren't they?

Here is the difference though: All children do experience some anxious feelings as a normal part of growing up, but there are occasions when those anxious and nervous emotions could be a sign of an underlying condition. One study discovered that out of 10,000 kids, <u>more than 30%</u> were dealing with an anxiety disorder, even before they were 18 years old.

If your child has an anxiety disorder, hoping that they will simply grow out of it is only going to lead to disappointment. As your child's brain continues to develop, there is a very strong possibility that these anxieties can intensify. When they do, it will lead to more serious, lifelong issues if your child does not learn how to cope with them. We are talking about depression, alcohol and substance abuse, daily struggles with school and life in general, eating disorders, and thoughts of suicide. Yes, there is a risk that your child may develop suicidal thoughts if their anxieties get out of control.

It may take some time for you to come to terms with the fact that your child needs help, but this is something that you are going to have to do sooner rather than later. Your child needs you, and possibly, they need professional help, depending on the severity of their anxiety.

Watching for Signs of Anxiety

One of the hardest challenges of parenting a child struggling with anxiety is that they will not tell you outright that they feel anxious. Younger kids do not even *know* what it is, let alone understand what they are dealing with. All they know is that they feel scared. You are going to have to watch out for signs of anxiety on your own. While not all of these signs necessarily mean that your child has anxiety, if you see them recurring on a regular basis, that is when you should start talking to your family doctor about your observations. Talk to a professional especially if these symptoms start having an impact on your child's everyday life.

Watch for the common lines that your child might utter, and if they occur too frequently, they could be a sign of anxiety:

- *"I'm not hungry."* (Sometimes, they would say this even though they have not eaten for hours.)
- *"My tummy hurts."*
- *"My head hurts."*
- *"I don't want to go to school."*
- *"Can I just stay at home?"*
- *"I'm sorry."* (Anxious kids can often worry about doing something wrong or bad, and they continuously apologize for even the smallest things.)

- *"I don't want to go; please don't make me."*
- *"Please don't leave me alone."*
- *"Can I stay home with you instead?"*
- *"I want to go home."*
- *"I can't do it Mummy/Daddy."*
- *"Can you do it for me?"*
- *"Are you angry with me?"* or *"Did I do something wrong?"* (Anxious kids always seek approval and reassurance.)
- *"I can't fall asleep."*
- *"I'm feeling tired."*
- *"I'm scared; what if something bad happens?"*
- *"I can't breathe."* (A symptom that manifests when they have a panic attack.)
- *"I can't make any friends."* Or, *"I don't have any friends."*

Becoming The Mind Reading Parent

Below are behavioral signs that may indicate the possibility of anxiety problems in your child. You should watch out for these as well.

- They often seem alone or sad.
- They cry a lot, especially the younger ones.
- They are quick to feel anger over the smallest issues.
- They easily become moody for no apparent reason.
- They have intense temper tantrums or complete emotional meltdowns.
- They seem irritable most of the time
- They are extremely sensitive and tend to take things personally.
- They overreact when they think that they are being criticized (even if the criticism is constructive).
- They cling to you even though you have only left them for a short time.

- They try to either hide or run away (the younger ones) to avoid certain situations.
- They feel agitated in certain situations.
- They often feel restless and find it difficult to keep still. A **study** of 128 children who were diagnosed with anxiety revealed that 74% of them reported that one of the primary symptoms they dealt with was restlessness.
- They have difficulty concentrating on their tasks.
- They feel easily afraid.
- They are easily fatigued.
- They get startled easily. One **study** conducted in 2008 and published in the *Depression and Anxiety Journal* showed that anxiety can cause a heightened "startled" response, especially during moments when a person feels mentally stressed.
- They struggle to make simple decisions.

- They frequently wake up at night, crying, because they had nightmares or bad dreams.
- They display signs of obsessive-compulsive behavior.
- They are too worried about their grades.
- They have trouble both falling asleep and staying awake.
- They display tendencies of being a perfectionist, constantly obsessing when something is not done "perfectly" the way they think it should be.

Younger children often find it easier to talk about their physical symptoms since they cannot quite understand emotions just yet, and if you observe any of these signs happening far too often, it may be time to consult your family doctor and get their perspective about it.

Chapter 7: Decluttering Media and Technology

We live in a world today where technology is unavoidable. There is no doubt that it has made our lives a lot easier and more convenient in many ways, but there is also no denying that technology does have a dark side that comes with it.

Depression, anxiety, and even suicide are on the rise among young people, with technology often being cited as one of the major contributors of this disturbing trend.

Could Technology be Causing Anxiety?

Technology has opened the doors for cyberbullies to wreak havoc on other young, vulnerable, and impressionable youth, and this is an apparent cause

Becoming The Mind Reading Parent

for concern. There have been far too many reports of young children being driven to all kinds of self-harm and violence against not just themselves but also others. This is an issue which was not prevalent several years ago. The worst outcome of such cases is, without a doubt, suicide.

Without the presence of cyberbullying, social media is already being blamed for the increased levels of anxiety among young children. An article in _The New York Times Magazine_ cited Stephanie Eken, a psychiatrist, who claimed that anxious teens were comparing themselves against their peers relentlessly, regardless of their backgrounds. The results were "uniformly distressing," according to her. Even the children were in agreement with Eken's analysis, claiming that while social media has become something that they cannot live without anymore, it was also a tool that drives them crazy at the same time.

Becoming The Mind Reading Parent

Further <u>research</u> indicates that those who spent too much time on the Internet or were addicted to its uses often turned to the online world to escape the negative emotions that they felt. These emotions include depression and anxiety. It was also revealed how internet use was associated with greater difficulties in emotional regulation. The researchers also discovered that, interestingly enough, the preference of turning to email, text, or instant messaging instead of face-to-face conversations may, in fact, increase the risk of vulnerability to social anxiety.

Technology certainly does seem to play a rather influential role in causing increased levels of anxiety among young children. <u>Researchers</u> discovered that, in Japan, a study involving teenagers (with a mean age of 18.4 years) revealed that when these teens did not receive an immediate response to their texts or instant messages, they fear that they were being ostracized. Therefore, the tendency to rely heavily on connecting with their social network potentially contributed to their anxiety.

Reconnecting with Your Digitally-Distracted Child

The next time you are out with your kids at a cafe or restaurant, take a subtle look around and observe just how many families are engaged in conversation with their kids and how many are glued to their devices. It is not just the kids who are intently focused on their mobile phones or tablets, but the parents are equally as guilty of doing the same thing. Instead of having meaningful conversations with each other, everyone seems to be more interested in what is going on in the online world.

Becoming The Mind Reading Parent

This trend does not seem to be happening just in restaurants, but even at home too. When was the last time you sat down for a meal together at the dining table with the whole family and everyone was talking to each other instead of scrolling through the latest social media updates? Technology is great and everything, but it can become the wedge that distances and disconnects the family as well. There is more <u>research</u> showing that kids who sit down and dine together with their whole family on most nights during the week have stronger emotional and mental health. If this is the case, then parents of kids with anxiety need to start connecting with their digitally-distracted children, now more than ever.

Good mental and emotional health habits begin at home, and parents can start taking steps toward this anxiety-coping measure by reconnecting with their digitally-distracted children.

Becoming The Mind Reading Parent

- Make it a family priority to spend more time together without devices or gadgets. Family dinners, family outings, movie night, or a game night are good activities – any activity that the whole family can get involved in, which includes more talking and less scrolling.

- When dining at a restaurant, make it a rule that all family members must tuck their phones away in their bags and start talking to each other instead. This includes the parents – put your phones away, and commit the next several minutes during your meal to your kids instead. Unless it is an absolute emergency, everything else can wait.

- Plan family activities that will get your teens or pre-teens out of their room and get together with the family. Anxious teens have a tendency to isolate and shut themselves away

in their bedroom, and this is a habit you want
to break.

- Set expectations and boundaries for
technology use at home. These expectations
and boundaries must be mutually agreed upon
by both kids and parents, so everyone is
happy, and your child will not resent the rules
you have set. For example, you could agree to
allow your kids 30 minutes of screen time, but
in return, they need to invest that same
amount of time away from the screen talking
to the family instead.

- Choose to mentor rather than to monitor.
You cannot keep your kids away from
technology forever, so instead, guide and
show them the proper and acceptable way to
use technology that benefits them. There is a
lot of good to be gained from using

technology, and you can teach your child how to self-regulate and self-advocate, so they understand what being a good digital citizen means. Your anxious child will not have to resort to becoming a tech shut-in.

Technology has its pros and cons; finding that balance between healthy usage and managing anxiety comes down to good communication skills. As long as you continue to keep your communication lines open and let your child know they can always talk to you anytime they need, you are fostering good communication at home.

Chapter 8: Nighttime Pillow Talk

If you are a parent of an anxious child, you probably know the nighttime drill by now. Getting your anxious kid to settle down at bedtime and keep them asleep throughout the night can be an exhausting challenge. Children need to get the proper amount of sleep each night, especially anxious kids. Without it, they will have a much harder time during the day trying to control their emotions. In that emotional state, their anxiety levels can quickly increase and get out of hand, and sleep-deprived children are more prone to behavioral and health-related problems, which include difficulty paying attention, trouble learning, and even obesity.

It is so crucial for your child to get the proper amount of sleep that is needed each night for their age group. What can you do to keep your anxious child calm and settled at night without having to stay awake the entire night yourself?

Strategies to Help Calm Your Child at Night

Having a regular bedtime routine and sleep schedule can play a significant role in helping your children get their much-needed restful sleep at night. Anxious kids need to have and maintain good sleep habits to help them stay asleep through the night. This also helps them wake up refreshed the next day. There is no hard-and-fast rule about the kind of bedtime habits you need to set since every child is different. You're going to need to find a routine that works best for your child and you, making it easier for them to stick to this routine without protest.

The first step toward helping your child stay calm at night is to pinpoint where their fear is coming from:

Becoming The Mind Reading Parent

What is causing the anxiety? Are they afraid of the monsters in their closet? The dark? Spiders? By identifying the exact cause of that fear, you can then begin working on several strategies to help your child overcome it so that they can sleep easier at night.

Some helpful strategies which might do the trick include the following:

- **Rearrange the room.** Is there a specific area in the room that your child is afraid of the most? Perhaps it is a corner that is darker than the rest. During the day, encourage your child to point out the areas of the room that scares them the most at night or makes them especially nervous. Ask your child what might help to make them feel better. Perhaps putting an extra night light in the darker corner may help? Or, you can move pieces of furniture around to make them feel safer.

Think about rearranging the room in a way that can be calmer and brighter for your child to ease their night terrors.

- **Talk to them about the importance of sleep.** Talk to your child about the importance of sleep and how they need it so their bodies and minds can grow strong and healthy. Setting regular bedtimes and wake-up times for the child helps them get into the habit and settle into a routine. It would also help if the whole family could support this by going to sleep at the same time.

- **Make nighttime routines fun.** Kids actually love routines and thrive on it because of the stability it provides. For anxious kids, knowing what to expect can be very helpful in keeping them relaxed and calm. A <u>study</u> showed that having a consistent routine helped children gain a sense of control over their environment, especially those who struggled with moderate-to-mild sleep problems.

- **Wear comfortable clothing.** Both adults and kids sleep much better at night when they are dressed in comfortable clothing. Is your child's sleep clothes too restrictive? Consider switching their pajamas with ones made of cool (or warm) and comfortable materials that help promote better sleep at night. Maybe you can pick out the clothes that your child feels excited to wear, so that they will look forward to it when they go to bed at night.

- **Create a soothing environment.** Playing soothing sounds or music at night can help your child drift off to sleep. Keep the volume low in the house, and dim the lights to create

the right ambiance for your child to drift off
to sleep peacefully.

- **Give them an item of security.** Your child
  may be anxious at the idea of being separated
  from you at night and being all alone by
  themselves. Having a security item, or
  something that makes them feel safe at night,
  can help them sleep better too – it could be a
  teddy bear, a doll they are attached to, or if
  they do not have an item of security just yet,
  give them one. Tell them a story about how
  this toy or item is going to protect them and
  keep them safe at night.

- **Read them a story.** A bedtime story is a
  child's favorite nighttime routine because they
  get to spend some time with the parent and
  listen to the voice that comforts them the
  most as they slowly drift off to sleep. Read a

nice, calming story. Keep your voice low and soothing, so your child feels peaceful and relaxed as they gently fall asleep.

- **Sing them to sleep.** If there is a particular song that your child loves and gives them great comfort, make it a habit to sing this song to them every night as they fall asleep. This would help soothe away any remaining troubles or worries they might have.

Important Words that Help You Connect with Your Child Before Bed

After a long and maybe anxious day for your child, it is time to wind down at night with the right bedtime pillow talk that can help you connect with your child. As the day draws to a close, you want to comfort and remind them of how much they are loved, even though they might have had a difficult day. That sense of security is what your anxious child needs right now, and a few, important words at night can make a dramatic difference in how they cope with their anxiety.

- **What was the best thing about today?** This teaches your child to focus on the positive and the things that make them happy, which instills within them the attitude of always being grateful. Given how <u>research</u> has shown that those who are genuinely grateful and appreciative tend to live happier lives, this is one habit you definitely want to impart to your child from the beginning.

- **What are you excited about tomorrow?** This is another great exercise in positivity that teaches your child to look forward to what is to come instead of fearing the unknown. Professor Martin Seligman, the author of "*The*

Optimistic Child," emphasized that optimism and hope could be a powerful tool against depression.

- **What would you like to talk about?** This encourages your child to open up about their feelings by letting them choose the topic of conversation.

- **Let's name all the people we love.** Going through a list of all the people who love them by naming them out loud reminds your child of the loving and supportive system that they have. Whenever they feel scared or alone, knowing that they are loved can help them find comfort in those moments of fear.

- **I love you very much.** A simple statement that reminds and reassures them of how much they are loved, and it is something every

Becoming The Mind Reading Parent

parent should say every night when you hug
and kiss your child goodnight.

Chapter 9: Morning Talks to Promote Positive Thinking

Every parent wants to see their child happy, but how many parents are actually engaging in habits that promote positive thinking in their child? People have a natural tendency to dwell more easily on the negative, even more so for a child who is dealing with anxiety. What you want to do now as part of your child's coping strategies is to help steer them away from that negative way of thinking. You want to help them develop habits at a young age that instill a positive attitude and an optimistic view of themselves and the world around them.

Establish a Routine that Encourages Positive Thinking

Helping your child develop a positive mindset from the beginning allows them to have a strong mental attitude that helps them perceive situations around them in a more constructive way. One study showed that children as young as 5 years old can grasp the concept of positive thinking. So, it is never too early to start working on building these habits with your child. When you nurture these habits in them from the very beginning, the power of positivity can be an excellent coping tool which helps your child develop the resilience that they need to overcome challenges without succumbing to negativity. There is no better time to set the tone for a good day ahead than first thing in the morning when the day begins anew.

Start your child's day on the right foot every morning with a routine that encourages positive thinking, from the moment they open their eyes and hop out of bed.

Becoming The Mind Reading Parent

- **Greet them with an enthusiastic smile.**
  Seeing your smiling, happy face first thing in
  the morning can set the mood of happiness
  from the beginning. Smiling is contagious, and
  when the first thing your child sees in the
  morning is a happy, smiling face followed by
  an enthusiastic "good morning!", they simply
  could not help smile in return and feel good
  about it.

- **Talk about what they can do to make
  today great.** Over breakfast, talk to your
  child about what they can do to make today a
  great day. Ask them what activities they would
  like to do together as a family or with their
  friends at school. Encouraging your child to
  design the kind of day that makes them happy
  will inspire them to focus on the positive
  experiences they can have.

- **Talk about their best self.** Every morning, encourage your child to talk about their very best self and picture them in their mind. You could do this over breakfast too or on the way to school by encouraging them to show an interest in themselves and getting them to think about what kind of people they want to be when they grow up. Ask them to talk about what makes them feel strong or what they do that makes them feel good about themselves. When children start feeling great about themselves, it helps them recapture their positive thoughts and hold onto the emotions that make them feel good.

- **Let's use positive words today.** Make it an exercise every morning when you and your child come up with a list of all the positive words they can use today to describe the different activities they are going to do. Expanding their vocabulary to include more positive words rather than negative ones strengthens within your child the ability to focus on the good instead of the bad. This is something that will be very useful in helping them alleviate their fears.

How to Foster Positive Thinking to Help Your Child Overcome Anxiety

A positive outlook in life can be just as contagious as a negative one, and your child can learn to develop the right kind of perspective if they have been given the right tools to do so from the beginning.

- **Be your child's role model.** Young children observe and notice everything that their parents do, so if you want to begin fostering positive thinking habits in your child, it needs to start with you. Your child is going to be confused if you tell them to think positively, but they see you doing the exact opposite. If you want to teach your child optimism, you need to be optimistic yourself. If you are going to teach them to see the bright side of things, you need to start doing the same.

- **Don't dismiss the bad stuff entirely.** Part of thinking positively is to acknowledge that sometimes, bad things also happen. Teach your child to recognize those moments when they do happen. Show them how to look at the silver lining in the situation and teach them that the lessons that arise from that experience will make them a better and stronger person.

Becoming The Mind Reading Parent

- **Foster an attitude of gratitude.** Encourage your child to talk about how happy they are after each activity they tackle throughout the day. Even simple things like *"I'm happy that I ate a delicious breakfast today," "I'm happy I got a hug from mummy this morning,"* or *"I'm happy I got to color a great picture today"* can teach your child to be grateful for all the things they did throughout the day. Inspire your child to vocalize their gratitude and reinforce those good feelings by saying, *"didn't it feel great to say that out loud?."* It also teaches them to develop a habit of learning to stop and appreciate the little things in life, which is the key to lifelong happiness.

- **Practice the loving kindness meditation.** Spend 2 minutes every morning and at the end of every day practicing the loving kindness meditation with your child. This would help them start or end the day filled with good feelings from within. Find a comfortable spot, sit down with them, and encourage them to close their eyes with you. Take a couple of deep, slow breaths while, together, you repeat positive affirmations, such as *"I am safe today," "I am happy today," "I am loved today."* This will help your child focus on both compassion and kindness, which are two very powerful qualities of positive thinking. There have been **studies** conducted that support the link between meditation and the power of positivity.

Chapter 10: Facing Their Fears (Gradually)

Everything seems bigger and scarier through the eyes of a child. As parents, we cannot even begin to imagine what that fear is doing to them, and it can be heartbreaking to know that your child is suffering. You may not always be able to take away their pain or shield them from everything out there in the big bad world, but what you can do is to work on helping them face their fears gradually. Give them a chance to grow into the strong, courageous, and independent individual you know that they can be, by giving them all the support they need. You *know* they can do it; now it is up to you to help them *believe* that they can.

Anxiety can be an awful thing for any child to deal with (even adults), but once your child learns how to cope, they will see that their fears are manageable as they grow older. Knowing that they have it in them to overcome anxiety can be a pretty powerful feeling. As a parent, there are several things you could do to encourage your child to develop a greater sense of confidence, courage, and independence. Some of these are described below.

- **Anxiety is *not* a sign that they're not okay.** Let them know that anxiety is a way for their brain to check in to make sure that everything is okay. Once they are older and able to understand more things, explain the fight or flight mechanism that reside in all our brains, and that worrying is our body's way of staying alert in case of any possible danger. When they see that there is no "danger" around them, they can begin to breathe consciously, telling their brains to calm down because everything is okay. Anxiety does not mean that there is something wrong with them, and they need to know this.

- **Let them know they're a warrior.** When they are old enough to understand, explain to your child how the human brain functions, where their anxiety is triggered in their brain, and that they are capable of great change. Each time they tell themselves they are strong, and they are a warrior, or whenever they overcome their fears, they are strengthening that part of the brain that helps them develop the courage they need. When your child has successfully overcome a fear, celebrate it with them, and encourage them to reinforce those feelings by repeating the words, "*I am strong, I am a warrior, I did it!*".

- **Encourage them to be proud of their bravery.** Anyone who is dealing with anxiety should be proud of how brave they are, and this is a concept you need to reinforce in your child. Let them know how much strength, courage, and determination it takes to face what they are afraid of, and you could not be more proud each time they push through a barrier that has been holding them back.

- **Remind them of their past victories.** In those moments when all they can think about is their worries or their fears, it can be challenging to recall moments when they were brave in the past. It could be difficult for them to remember how they overcame some of the fears that used to trouble them. When that happens, talk them through it – remind them of all the times they were scared, just like how they are now, and they still managed to overcome it anyway. Thoughts can be powerful things, and drawing memories of the moments when they were brave can help your child gradually build up the courage they need to overcome the next hurdle in front of them.

- **Let them know that anxiety has given them a special gift.** Being afraid may not seem much like a gift, but it is. Give your child a new perspective on their anxiety by letting them know how this feeling has given them a very special and unique gift – this gift is their ability to understand what someone else might be going through when they are afraid, too. Thanks to this ability, they can easily imagine what the person must feel, having felt those emotions themselves. And now, they have this empathy that allows them to understand and help others in a similar position. Being able to help someone else will make them feel like a hero.

- **Talk to them about the importance of caring for both the body and the mind.** If you taught your child at a young age that taking care of the mind is just as important as taking care of their bodies, they would carry that habit with them all the way into adulthood. Most parents tend to place more emphasis on talking to their kids about how important it is to take care of their bodies – a habit even a lot of adults are guilty of. Making good mental health habits and building mental strength priorities for the whole family will reinforce within your child that they should not neglect their mental health. In addition, the child would know that sometimes, it is okay to talk to a doctor who can help take care of their mental health if needed. Tell them that this is just like going to the dentist to take care of their teeth.

Becoming The Mind Reading Parent

- **Make it a priority to talk about emotions.**
  It is not always a comfortable subject, but
  making it a priority to have regular talks about
  emotions is part of teaching them how to
  identify and cope with their feelings. You
  send your kids to school to prepare them
  academically for the world, but what about
  preparing them emotionally for all of life's
  challenges? Parents need to begin investing
  time and making it a priority to talk about
  uncomfortable or awkward feelings. A survey
  that was conducted on 1,502 students in
  college revealed that 60% of these students
  were not emotionally prepared for the
  challenges they felt and that they wished that
  their parents had perhaps spent more time
  teaching and guiding them how to deal with
  emotions like anxiety. Your kids are going to
  grow up and go to college one day, and if they
  do not learn the coping skills they need from

the beginning, they will struggle with it throughout their life. Start having regular, even daily discussions about emotions. Ask your child how they feel, and help them put a name to the emotions they experience. Proactively teaching them instead of ignoring their feelings helps them manage and express their feelings in healthier ways.

Chapter 11: Eat, Pray, Sleep, and Exercise

Developing healthy, lifelong habits are vital to helping your anxious child grow into a confident, strong adult who will be able to cope with all the challenges that life throws their way. Ask any parent what they want for their child in the future, and the answer will almost always be: Happiness and success.

There is no shortage of advice on how to raise successful and smart kids, but what about raising kids who are *happy?* It can sometimes be challenging to balance between what is good for them and what makes them happy, but these two traits do not always have to be mutually exclusive. Happier children are more likely to be successful anyway, even with anxiety.

Eating Right for a Healthy Mind

Eating dinner together gives your child the gift of being able to bond with the family and people who love them the most. This is precious quality time that all anxious kids need to have so that they would feel loved and supported. Besides eating together, make it a habit to eat more nutritious food that will be essential to the growth and development of a healthy body and mind. Encourage the following good eating habits in your child during mealtimes:

- Teach your child how to eat slowly and mindfully, so that they can enjoy the taste of the food. This way, they also get to learn how to distinguish between hunger and fullness.

- Give your child's brain time to register its fullness by asking them to wait 10-15 minutes before asking for seconds.

Becoming The Mind Reading Parent

- Involve your child in the grocery shopping. Let them pick out their own nutritious food by asking them what they think is suitable for their bodies and minds to grow strong and healthy. If they learn to pick the right foods from the beginning, they will carry this habit later on and continue to maintain good eating habits.

- Encourage your child to stay hydrated and drink enough water during the day by turning it into a fun challenge. Fill up several bottles of water (enough for the required amount they need), and challenge them to see how many they can finish in a day.

Sleeping Soundly at Night

Besides maintaining a consistent sleep schedule and bedtime routine, other healthy sleep habits that you could instill in your child include the following:

- Encourage them not to go to bed hungry. Ask them if they are feeling hungry or if they would like a glass of milk before bed, but avoid offering heavy meals just before bedtime.

- Spend 30 minutes of quiet time together, either reading a book or doing a quiet activity before bed to help them begin winding down their energy levels. This would also be an excellent time to have conversations with your child about the topic discussed in Chapter 8.

- Discourage the use of screen time at least 30 minutes before bed.

- Keep your child's room at just the right temperature to encourage better sleep at night. A room that is too hot or too cold can have an effect on their ability to sleep continuously at night.

- Ensure that your child's mattress is comfortable enough to provide them the right kind of support they need for a good night's sleep.

The Gift of Exercise

Exercise is not just about running outside and playing, although that is certainly good for their physical development. There are different kinds of physical and mental activities that you could practice with them, and these are just as beneficial as running around outdoors for exercise:

Becoming The Mind Reading Parent

- Get them involved in household chores around the house, doing it with you or with their siblings. This gives them the gift of collaborating and working well with others.

- Exercising their social skills matters just as much as physical exercise does. Researchers from Duke University and Pennsylvania State University tracked a **study** of more than 700 respondents between kindergarten and 25 years of age across the United States. They discovered that there was a significant correlation when it came to the social skills they developed as kindergarteners and the success they experienced as adults later on.

- Improving emotional intelligence gives your child the gift of learning one of the most valuable skills a person can possess when it comes to regulating their emotions. Allow them to exercise emotional intelligence by teaching them to validate and label their feelings whenever they experience intense emotions.

- Enroll your child in an activity that they are interested in. Gymnastics, martial arts, or dance classes can make exercise a fun activity and a habit that your child is likely to carry on to their later years if they find it enjoyable.

- Make exercise routines a priority by being a model in keeping a regular exercise schedule for yourself. Exercises can easily be performed in the comfort of your own home, following along several videos or apps. Doing it with your child is a great way to bond together.

And Finally, the Power of Prayer

Praying together every night as a family teaches your child the gift of forgiveness, compassion, and gratitude. If you are not particularly religious, that is okay because you can do this similar exercise by getting your child to recall all the things they have to be grateful for in their life. The power of prayer has the same impact as the power of positive affirmations, and while we often think affirmations work best for adults, they do remarkable wonders in helping shift your child's perception when this practice becomes a habit.

Prayer and positive affirmations remind both parent and child that, despite all the big, bad, scary things out there in the world, there are still plenty of things to be grateful for. One is being grateful for another day that the family is safe, happy, and healthy. You can also teach them to be thankful for another day that they spent with the ones they love. Ask them to be grateful for being strong and having the chance to conquer their fears. The power of prayer, positivity, and gratitude are all interconnected, and they all work together to boost your child's self-esteem. They can encourage them to feel good about themselves despite their anxiety. They remind your child that they are good enough just the way they are, and even if it takes a while for them to overcome their fears, they will always have the love and support of their family to help them through it all no matter what.

Conclusion

Thank you for making it to the end of this book. Let's hope it was informative and that it provided you the tools that you need to help your child cope with anxiety.

Your role as a parent of an anxious child is one of the most important responsibilities you will have in helping them manage their anxiety. Whether they are young children or teenagers trying to work through their worries, parents play a fundamental role in teaching their children how to cope with their emotions. Parents help them face what scares them, take risks within reason, and eventually, gain the confidence they need to surpass obstacles.

Parenting a child who is dealing with anxiety can be challenging, but you do not have to do it alone. There are plenty of other resources and helplines you could reach out to. The best thing you could do for your child, besides helping them to work through their anxiety using the strategies in this book, is to equip yourself with as much knowledge and information about child anxiety as possible. Overcoming anxiety together with your child is going to take time. You need to be patient, remain calm, and understand that you may need to invest a considerable amount of time in helping your child cope with their worries before you start to see a noticeable, positive difference.

All the knowledge, tools, and strategies you have picked up in this book are going to help you manage your anxious child. Having the right information may mean the difference between having a child who grows into a happy, confident adult and one that brings their anxiety into adulthood. Your goal as a parent is to see your child handle any challenges in a healthy manner rather than see them shut down as a result of their inability to overcome anxiety.

Becoming The Mind Reading Parent

It all comes down to how both parent and child work together to overcome anxiety. When your child learns how to keep their fears under control, a happy childhood is possible despite having an anxiety disorder.

Becoming The Mind Reading Parent

We also appreciate honest book reviews from our readers.

Connect with us on our Facebook page

www.facebook.com/bluesourceandfriends and stay tuned

to our latest book promotions and free giveaways.